Fractured Fables

A
Silverline™
B O O K S
PRODUCTION
A Division of
Shadowline™/***image***®

Edited by
Jim Valentino
and Kristen K. Simon

Book Design by
Jim Valentino

Cover Illustration by
Michael and Laura Allred
from a sketch by Jim Valentino

Cover Design and Graphics by
Tim Daniel

Special thanks to
Marc Lombardi

Jim Valentino
Publisher

for image:
Eric Stephenson
publisher
Todd Martinez
sales & licensing
Betsy Gomez
pr & marketing
Branwyn Bigglestone
accounts manager
Sarah deLaine
administrative assistant
Tyler Shainline
production manager
Drew Gill
art director
Jonathan Chan
Monica Howard
Vincent Kukua
production artists

FRACTURED FABLES
ISBN: 978-1-60706-269-1

Ages 12+

PRINTED IN SOUTH KOREA   First Printing, July, 2010

Table of Contents

The Silly Statue

An Alice in Wonderland Story

Dara Naraghi
(writer/letterer)

Grant Bond
(artist)

ONE DAY, IN WONDERLAND...

OH MY, A STATUE OF *THE QUEEN OF HEARTS.*

WHAT ARE *YOU* STARING AT?

EEEP!

OH ALICE, YOU'RE SO *EASY* TO *SCARE!*

THE *CHESHIRE CAT!* I SHOULD HAVE KNOWN.

WHAT ARE YOU *DOING* UP THERE?

OH, JUST HAVING SOME *FUN* BY MAKING THE QUEEN LOOK *SILLY.*

HOW DO YOU MEAN?

WELL, *FOR EXAMPLE,* I CAN GIVE HER...

HEE HEE

THE QUEEN WOULD BE SO *MAD* IF SHE SAW YOU DOING THIS.

SPEAKING OF WHICH...

OH NO! THE QUEEN!

WHAT IS ALL THIS *COMMOTION* ABOUT?

ALICE! WHAT ARE YOU DOING?

UM, NOTHING YOUR HIGHNESS. JUST...UH, *ADMIRING* YOUR STATUE.

HMMPH
I DO NOT LIKE THE LOOK ON MY *FACE* AT ALL.

NO, THIS SIMPLY WON'T DO.

ONCE UPON A TIME THERE WAS A BOY NAMED JACK.

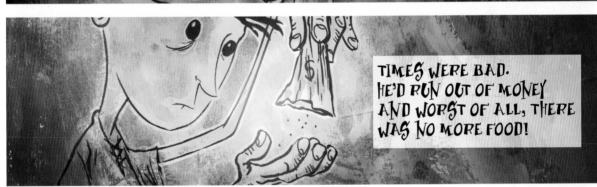

TIMES WERE BAD. HE'D RUN OUT OF MONEY AND WORST OF ALL, THERE WAS NO MORE FOOD!

SO JACK HIT THE ROAD. HE TRAVELLED FAR AND WIDE...HE WAS SO HUNGRY!

FINALLY, HE CAME ACROSS A CASTLE...

Great idea!

HEY Look! An Englishman!

TRIP!

OOOOOOFFFF!

CRASH!

IT TURNS OUT, WITH A BIT OF MINT SAUCE, GIANTS TASTE FANTASTIC!

Pleased to meet you but I've gotta hurry on through the woods to *Grandma's.*

Er...and where might that be, pumpkin?

And I'm sure her Grandma will have lots of *ketchup* and *pickles* and... hmm.

Farewell, dear child!

WOOOOSH

Cool!

At the end of this path, *silly.*

Goodbye Mister Wombat!

GRANDMA'S

I *must* get there *first!* That'll be the *perfect* place to trap and devour my unexpected *culinary treat!*

Oh, *LOOK!* There's some lovely *flowers* over there! Why don't you *pick* some for Grandma?

Ah, *here* we are! Easy peasy!

Marvellous! The *aged relative* appears to be *absent!*

I know! I'll *disguise* myself as the old trout! And, *the second* that little *Red Riding Hood* is within *snapping* distance of my *teeth,* she'll be in my *belly* before you can say *Bob's your uncle!*

Let's see...*yes!* This *blanket* and this *towel* should do the *trick!*

She's only a *silly little girl,* when all's said and done!

18

19

20

by Terry Moore

There once was a king with two beautiful daughters, and another one named Gertie. For some reason, Gertie didn't look like the rest of the family, instead bearing a strong resemblance to Skippy, the court jester. All the same, the good king loved his three daughters equally, because he had a kind heart and weak eyes.

One day, Gertie was standing by a well near the castle stables, texting a friend, when a loud noise startled her so that she dropped her phone. Plop! Plop! Crash! Splash! went the phone, down the well, into the muddy water where all the mosquitoes lived. Oh, the princess was mad! She cried. She wailed. She even said a bad word that no nice girl should ever say unless she catches her husband making a fool of himself with a tart half his age.

Gertie was seriously considering diving down the well after her phone when, all of a sudden, a voice said, "You have a potty mouth. But those legs... HarrrUMBah!"

When the princess turned there was... a fat little toad in a plaid suit, smoking a cigar and looking at her the way a moose looks at a Mini Cooper. You know the look I'm talking about.

Gertie sniffed and turned back to the well. "Go away, toad. I have a terrible problem and you can't help me."

The toad puffed on his cigar. "Dropped your phone down the well, didn't ya? Wish you could get it back, don't ya? I dare say none of the king's stable boys will go down that well for you. But I would... for a price."

"You've got a deal!" said the princess, grabbing the toad by his shorts.

"Wait! Don't you want to hear the price?" he squealed.

"Whatever! Just do it!" said the princess, and she heaved the toad into the well.

Reluctantly, Gertie opened the door, let the toad in, and asked him to state his price. The toad cleared his throat and said with a smile, "Oh princess fair, all I ask in return for my bravery is a single kiss, from you."

The princess howled, "Oh ho ho ho... NO WAY! I am NOT kissing a toad!"

"Gertie!" the king barked. And that was that. The princess threw down her napkin. "Fine! Whatever pleases His Loudness!" Gertie stomped from the room, motioning for the toad to follow. "Come on, toad!"

Because the king was rich and the castle large, it was a long walk to Gertie's room. Gertie took big, angry, oddly uneven steps, so that it was all the toad could do to keep up. But, scuttling behind her, he was all smiles. "Princess, I promise... you won't regret this."

"Shut up, toad," the princess snarled as they made their way through the vomitorium. No, it wasn't the prettiest route, but it was the shortest and the princess wanted to get this over with as soon as possible.

The toad soon tossed the phone up to the princess, then asked for a helping hand out of the well. "Forget it, sucker!" Gertie said with a laugh, then hopped back to the castle for snacks and a nasal rinse.

Later that night, Gertie was eating dinner with the royal family when a knock came on the door. "Gertie, see who that is," said the king. When Gertie opened the door, there stood the toad, mostly dry, puffing on a new cigar. "Hello, princess..." he began, before Gertie SLAM!med the door in his face.

"Who was that?" the king asked.

"Just some horrible toad I met at the stables this afternoon," said Gertie.

Then Gertie told her father everything that happened at the well. Everything except for the bad word, of course. The king frowned, then burped in Gertie's general direction and ordered her to let the toad in. "He has earned his reward and you have as good as promised him whatever he asks. And so it shall be," said the king.

bed, was a handsome prince. He smiled at Gertie with perfect white teeth. "Surprise!" he said.

Gertie was so shocked, she screamed bloody murder. The royal guards—who always stood outside her door—immediately burst into the room and speared the prince to the wall.

Once in her room, the princess plopped onto her bed and pointed to her cheek, "Go ahead then. Kiss me and be on your way."

"Oh no," said the toad, "the deal is you have to kiss me! And it has to be a proper kiss, on the lips. That's the deal or I will go to your father and tell him the bad word you said at the well."

At this Gertie's eyes grew wide with fear. So she took a deep breath, closed her eyes and puckered up.

KISS!

When Gertie opened her eyes the toad was gone. Instead, kneeling before her on the

With his last breath, the prince murmured something about a witch's spell and a wedding. But then again, maybe it was just one of those awful noises the body makes when it is speared to a wall.

The E...

Oh, also... Gertie had the whole mess cleaned up and never told her father what happened to the toad who came to dinner. But every day, at the same time, Gertie wobbles out to the stables and throws a phone down the well. No other toads have come forth and none of the stable boys dare ask her what in the world she's doing.

The End.

mary had a little spam

story-kristen k. simon pencils-jim valentino inks-aaron valentino colors-paul john little

MARY HAD A LITTLE SPAM
HER EXCITEMENT WAS QUITE LOW

IT DIDN'T REALLY
TASTE THAT GREAT

BUT SHE'D BEEN
CURIOUS, THOUGH.

SHE FRIED IT IN
A PAN ONE DAY

WHICH TASTED PRETTY COOL. BUT
IT MADE HER BROTHERS LAUGH AT HER...

... AND TREAT HER O, SO CRUEL.

SO SHE SADLY THREW IT OUT, BUT THE TASTE STILL LINGERED CLEAR

AND HAUNTED HER WITH DELICIOUS THOUGHTS OF SPAM CUBES ON A SPEAR.

WHY DOES SPAM INTRIGUE YOU SO?

DID HER MOCKING BROTHER CRY.

BECAUSE IT'S SOMETHING DIFFERENT, YOU KNOW

MARY DID REPLY.

THE END

ROW ROW ROW

SHANNON WHEELER

YOUR BOAT

GENTLY DOWN THE STREAM

THE SECRET PRINCESS SOCIETY

Marie Cruz - writer   Whilce Portacio - art

Going to Lionhead Dance Camp was a dream come true for Mimi. She would be truly happy if she didn't have her little sister to look after. Mimi had been worried that Meg would be following her around the whole time. That was because Meg thought her big sister was cool and wanted to do everything she did.

But not this time.

Mimi and her cousin, Justin, had just finished rehearsing their tap dance routine when the ballroom dance group let out on the other side of the studio. A group of giggling girls in their billowing practice skirts spilled out of the door in a swirl of color.

Mimi nudged Justin and said, "Here come the Princesses."

When Meg started her ballroom dance class, she had been thrilled to find out that they would be performing the Waltz of the Twelve Dancing Princesses.

Her new friends were just as excited so they banded together to form the Secret Princess Society. Justin thought it was silly. Mimi thought it was cute even though her sister didn't invite her to join.

Meg and her friends whispered and giggled so much they didn't notice Mimi and Justin coming toward them. Just as they came up to the group, Meg whispered, "Don't worry, I won't tell my sister."

Mimi couldn't believe what she just heard because her little sister told her everything. That was just how she was. So Mimi couldn't resist teasing her sister and asked, "Tell me what, Meg?"

Meg, bouncing with excitement, looked from her friends to Mimi and back again. "Oh, Mimi, guess what?" asked Meg, already forgetting her promise, "We're going to have a sleepover!"

It was Mimi's turn to look surprised. She thought, Oh, so it was "Mimi" now instead of "Ate". She missed hearing Meg use the Filipino word for big sister.

"There's no such a thing as a sleepover at camp."

"Oh, yes there is! It's going to be in Jenna's room and only Secret Princesses are allowed! Oops, sorry," said Meg. The other girls smiled at her but said nothing. Then they all skipped back into the studio behind them with Meg in tow.

Mimi tried not to feel bad. She thought she would feel glad that Meg had friends. But the truth was she felt sad and maybe a little jealous. She thought that Meg would always be there. Mimi wondered if her sister still looked up to her.

Mimi stared at Meg's empty bed and wondered if her little sister was having fun. She had wanted to tell Meg not to go but she couldn't come up with a good reason to make her stay.

Her parents made her promise to keep an eye on her little sister, to keep her close when they didn't have dance class. Mimi hoped she wasn't breaking her promise.

After all, Meg's sleepover was just on the other side of the building.

Between the pillow and her cheek was the silver medallion her grandmother had given her before leaving for camp.

Justin and Meg each had one too, but they didn't like wearing necklaces.

Mimi brought the pendant close to her face so she could see the pretty flower design on the front.

Her grandmother said it was a special pendant that would protect her from harm. She turned the pendant over to see the reflection of the moon on its polished surface.

Mimi suddenly heard a thump and a giggle outside her window.

She thought she imagined it until she heard another giggle. She crept to the window to investigate.

Out on the lawn were Meg and her friends walking toward the forest. They each carried a lighted candle that looked like little stars dancing on the grass as they walked.

What were they doing outside?

Mimi tried to push the window open but it was stuck. She wanted to bang on the window to get their attention, to let them know that she caught them sneaking out. But they were too far away. She had to go after them. After putting on a robe, she ran to Justin's room to wake him.

Mimi and Justin found the side door unlocked. They slipped out into the chilly night. Mimi ran toward the glow of candle light with Justin close behind her. The medallion bounced on her chest as she ran.

31

In the distance, Mimi saw the twelve Secret Princesses entering the forest one by one. Each girl plucked a flower from a low bush with glossy green leaves. Mimi had gone hiking with Justin on this trail many times but never noticed the bush there before.

The flowers were so white they seemed to glow like the moon. Meg, in her sparkling recital dress, was the last to pick a flower. She tucked it behind her ear as the girls in front of her did. Then Meg stepped into the forest just as Mimi and Justin caught up with them.

"Meg! Hey, Meg!" Mimi couldn't believe that Meg would ignore her but she did. Meg continued to follow the girl in front of her. Mimi walked along-side her sister but Meg didn't seem to notice her. She tried to talk to each of the girls in line but they paid no attention to her.

Mimi turned around and saw Justin pluck a flower from the bush. She watched in fascination as he held the flower in front of him and began to walk in the same direction as Meg and her friends.

The flowers looked like tiny stars against its dark green leaves. Its perfume enveloped her, inviting her to come closer. Mimi had seen the flower before! It was the same flower on her medallion. She plucked one.

A path appeared before her. It led to a large tree. Thin branches snaked down into the ground around it. Surrounding the base of the tree were small green mounds that made the hairs on Mimi's arms stand on end and the medallion felt like a piece of ice on her chest.

Meg and her friends chanted "tabi tabi po" in their high sing-song voices as they walked along the path that wove between the mounds toward the tree. The massive trunk had a cleft as tall and wide as a door. One by one, the princesses stepped into the opening in the tree. "Come on," whispered Mimi, holding the flower in front of her.

She fell in step behind Meg.

Justin and Mimi followed
Meg into the tree.

The walls were covered with
white scaly fungus. A tunnel
spiraled downward and
opened into a carpeted hallway
lined with marble columns
and portraits of kings and queens.

At the end of the hall stood
twelve young (handsome?) princes with their hands out-
stretched toward Meg and her friends (they really seemed like
princesses now!).

The couples turned and paraded into a grand ballroom
lit with hundreds of candles. They followed the last couple,
imitating their walk and posture.

On each side of the room were rows of golden tables
with silver plates of fruit and glasses filled with honey colored
liquid.

At the end of the room was a long banquet table with
platters of roasted meat and cheeses and at its center sat a
big man dressed like a king.

He beckoned to the couples with a smile on his long
horse-like face.

Mimi and Justin jumped behind the first table as they entered.

"What are we going to do?" whispered Mimi, sneaking a peek at the dance floor.

The princes and their princesses paraded before this king. They bowed and curtsied then twirled onto the dance floor. Music played and the twelve couples twirled across the polished floor.

"Watch and see what happens, I guess," said Justin, staring at the plate of fruit on the table. He reached out to take one but Mimi smacked his hand away.

The not-so-handsome princes were clumsy dancers. They stepped on dresses and toes but the princesses didn't seem to notice. There was something strange about their faces too. Eyes and noses seemed to slide out of place and back again.

The dance ended.
        The princes led their partners to the banquet table. Mimi wanted to get a closer look.
        She tried to sneak over to the next table when she tripped and fell. Her medallion snapped off its chain and rolled onto the dance floor. She scrambled over to it as fast as she could and snatched it up. Mimi polished the pendant on her robe and opened her hand to have a look at it before dropping it into her pocket.

Mimi stared into the medallion in confusion.

She saw herself reflected there but something was wrong.

The room did not look the same. The reflection didn't show candles, golden tables or silver plates of fruit. Instead of candles she saw sticks covered with something bright and writhing. The tables and chairs were raw stumps of wood. When she tilted the medallion, she saw wooden cages suspended on ropes above each set of rough wooden tables and chairs.

Mimi's heart pounded in her chest and tilted the medallion again.

The princes were not princes after all. Their faces melted away, eyes, ears, and noses sliding off, revealing what they truly were.

Dwarves!
She wasn't sure she wanted to know what the king looked like but she knew she had to look.

Mimi turned her back to the king and searched for his reflection in the pendant.
What she saw made her knees tremble.

The king was a creature with a head like a horse but instead of dull square teeth, he had long sharp ones.
His pointed tongue flicked out of his mouth as he watched the princesses fill their plates with the food on the banquet table.
Mimi suddenly understood what the cages were for!

With the medallion still clutched in her hand, Mimi crawled back to where Justin was hiding.

"This whole place is just a mirage!
I think that monster is going to trap Meg and the others.
We have to find a way to break this spell and get them out of here," said Mimi.

"What are we going to do?
We don't know what made the spell so how are we
going to break it? Do you think it has anything to
do with these?" said Justin, grimacing at the flowers
they were holding.

"Justin! That's it! You're a genius," said Mimi and gave her
cousin a big hug. She grabbed the flower in Justin's hand. Both
flowers were dropped onto the floor and crushed under her feet.

The room wavered in front of them, the ballroom changing to
an underground cavern.
The faces of the king and princes melted, their disguises slip-
ping and sliding.
"Let's rescue our twelve dancing princesses," said Mimi.

Justin and Mimi ran around the ballroom, snatching the
flowers out of the princess's hair. They threw all the flowers to the
ground and stomped on them. Each princess blinked rapidly, the
magic spell broken.
The girls looked around and stared at the dwarves as
they tried to keep their princely disguises intact.

Meg giggled.
The rest of the girls began to laugh.
The horse king, the dwarves and the cavern disappeared.

They all stood on the lawn just outside their dormitory.
The moon was still high and bright in the sky.
Meg hugged her big sister and cried, "Ate!"

Back in their room, Mimi still couldn't sleep. She wondered if the forest held other secrets and imagined what they might be.

Meg, on the other hand, was tucked in her bed, fast asleep, wearing her own medallion.

Mimi was happy to have her little sister there with her.
After what happened tonight, she knew that Meg would probably stick to her like glue for the rest of dance camp and would want to do everything her "Ate" did.

And Mimi didn't mind this one single bit.

ELF NETWORK NEWS: SPECIAL REPORT

A RISE IN THE EARTH'S TEMPERATURE IS CAUSING A SERIOUS MELTDOWN.

CHUCK MCKRAKEN — ENN
UPDATES: SCOTCH TAPE MADE FROM REAL SCOTCH!

UH...SO MUCH SO THAT WE NEED MORE SPONGES TO MOP UP AROUND...

GOT SPONGE?

CHUCK MCKRAKEN — ENN
WATERPROOF WRAPPING PAPER EPIC FAIL!

HURRY, SEND BUCKETS, BILGE PUMPS, MOPS...EVEN KITTY LITTER FOR THE LOVE OF...

...A LIFE JACKET!!!

CHUCK MCKRAKEN — ENN
ENN LOOKING FOR NEW OFFICE SPACE

TROUBLE AT THE North Pole
by Shane White

A SIGNAL WAS SENT OUT WEEKS AGO FROM THE NORTH POLE. THE ICE IS MELTING AND CHRISTMAS MIGHT JUST BE UNDERWATER.

THE REAL QUESTION IS WHAT IS THE EFFECT AND WHY IS IT HAPPENING? WE'LL EXPLORE THIS MYSTERY IN GREATER DETAIL IN THIS LIVE REPORT.

FLAPPITY FLAP FLAP

CALL IT EVOLUTION OR PURE DESPERATION BUT THE ONLY GOOD THING TO COME OUT OF THIS NATURAL DISASTER IS PENGUINS ARE LEARNING TO FLY. ROGER?

DARRYL OVENMITT — ENN

WITH A SHORTAGE OF SEALS, POLAR BEARS ARE LICKING... ER...LOOKING AT OTHER FOOD SOURCES FOR WINTER. BUT WILL THERE BE A WINTER AT THE RATE WE'RE GOING?

SLURP

PSST...GET ME OUT OF HERE?

ROGER DODGER — ENN

NOW THE HUMAN ELEMENT OF OUR UNFORTUNATE TALE. *NICK AGLUK*, AN INUIT NATIVE WHOSE LIFE DEPENDS ON SEALS FOR FOOD AND SNOW FOR SHELTER, IS BEING FORCED TO CHANGE HIS WAY OF LIFE.

Sniff Sniff

NICK AGLUK- INUIT DAY TRADER

IN THESE MOST TAXING OF TIMES ONE MAN HAS RISEN FROM THE TROUBLED WATERS TO *HELP* IN THIS RESCUE EFFORT.

I KNOW, THE CAMERAS ARE GOING TO ADD TEN POUNDS BUT I'VE ALREADY LOST FIVE UNDER THESE LIGHTS!

TELL MY AGENT IF THIS NORTH POLE THING DOESN'T WORK OUT...

SIR, YOU'RE ON!

PLEDGE NOW

...CALL YA BACK, SWEETIE!

FRIENDS, I'M JUST... I'M JUST GOING TO PUT IT OUT THERE. *WE* NEED *YOUR* HELP IN A BAD WAY.

LITTLE FROSTY, HERE NEEDS YOUR HELP IN A BAD WAY. I'M NOT ASKIN' I'M BEGGIN' YA.

BA-BLOOP

MY ELVES NEED YOUR HELP TOO. THESE LIL' FELLERS ARE UNSTOPPABLE BUT REALLY...

...WHO WANTS SOGGY PRESENTS THAT SMELL LIKE SHARKBUTT?

I KNOW I DON'T!

SO HERE'S WHAT YOU DO IF YOU KIDS WANNA SAVE CHRISTMAS LIKE IN THOSE TERRIBLE MOVIES THAT I HAVE NEVER BEEN ASKED TO STAR IN...AHEM...SURPRISE YOUR PARENTS WITH REAL ENGAGING TALK ABOUT WHY WE NEED TO STOP GLOBAL WARMING.

LOOK, WE GOT STAFF BACK HERE STANDING BY TO TAKE YOUR PLEDGE. WE'RE NOT ASKING FOR MUCH BUT GIVE 'TIL IT HURTS.

SNO-CONES, POPSICLES FUDGESICLES, HECK THROW A TRAY OF ICE CUBES IN AN ENVELOPE AND SAVE YOURSELF A PHONE-CALL. YOU KNOW THE ADDRESS.

BETTER YET, IF YOU CAN GET YOUR HANDS ON A YETI I HEAR THEIR BREATH HAS CAUSED RECORD-BREAKING BLIZZARDS IN THE YUKON TERRITORY. *DO THAT* AND *I'LL* THROW A LITTLE SOMEPIN SOMEPIN IN YOUR STOCKING, GET ME?

THAT CONCLUDES OUR SPECIAL REPORT ON THE NORTH POLE DISASTER NOW IN PROGRESS. FOR ELF NETWORK NEWS I'M CHUCK McKRAKEN DRYING OUT SOME-WHERE ON TOP OF THE WORLD.

RumpleStiltSkin

BY Doug TenNapel

THERE WAS ONCE A GREEDY KING WHO WALKED ABOUT HIS KINGDOM LOOKING FOR A WOMAN TO MARRY.

THE KING MET A FOOLISH MAN WHO TRIED TO IMPRESS THE KING BY TELLING LIES.

SHE DOESN'T LOOK LIKE MUCH, BUT SHE CAN TURN HAY INTO GOLD!

IS THAT TRUE?

UH-HUH.

ACHOO!

THE KING GREW SUSPICIOUS THAT THE MAN WAS LYING TO TRICK HIM INTO MARRYING HIS DAUGHTER.

GOLD, AYE? I HAVE A PLAN!

GREAT LET'S HEAR IT!

SNIiiiFF

WELL, THAT GIRL CAME A LONG WAY FROM BEING A MORONIC YOUNG LADY TO BEING A MORONIC QUEEN OF THE LAND.

DUH, LIFE IS SO EASY!

HI. REMEMBER ME?

DUH, WHO ARE YOU? HOW DID YOU GET PAST MY ROYAL GUARDS?!

IT'S SIMPLE. I'M A MAGIC LITTLE MAN. IN CASE YOU FORGOT, THE KING ONLY MARRIED YOU BECAUSE HE THOUGHT YOU COULD TURN HAY INTO GOLD... WHICH ONLY I CAN DO... AND I ONLY DID IT TO GET YOUR SON.

BUT IF YOU TAKE MY SON, THE KING WILL BEHEAD ME! AND WITH NO HEAD, HOW WILL I THINK?

DON'T GET ALL BENT OUTTA SHAPE! I'M A REASONABLE, FUNNY LITTLE, MAGIC MAN.

I'LL LET YOU KEEP YOUR SON, IF YOU CAN GUESS MY NAME!

THIS IS WHEN YOU TRY TO GUESS MY NAME.

OH.

IS IT SAM?

NO. TRY AGAIN.

OKAY, IS IT UH, SAM?

NO. IT'S NOT SAM. YOU ALREADY GUESSED THAT. I'LL GIVE YOU ONE MORE TRY!

UHHH, UMM, UHHH, IS IT SAM?

NO, DINGUS. MY NAME STILL ISN'T SAM!

NOW IF YOU'LL EXCUSE ME, I'LL BE TAKING MY SON. YOU CAN TRY TO GUESS MY NAME AGAIN TOMORROW.

GOO.

BY THE WAY, I'M GONNA NAME HIM BARNEY! GOOD-NIGHT.

OH, BOO-HOO! HE CAN'T DO THIS...

...HE CAN'T NAME HIM BARNEY!

THE NEXT DAY, THE LITTLE MAGIC MAN LEARNED HOW HARD IT IS TO TAKE CARE OF A BABY.

HOW AM I SUPPOSED TO FIGURE OUT ALL OF THESE STUPID CAR-SEAT STRAPS?!

GOO!

THAT NIGHT HE CAME BACK TO THE GIRL, HOPING SHE WOULD GUESS HIS NAME!

OKAY, IF YOU CAN GUESS MY NAME, YOU CAN HAVE YOUR BRAT-- I MEAN, YOUR SON BACK.

IS IT SA-

IT'S NOT STINKIN' SAM!

IT RHYMES WITH SHMUMPLESTILTSKIN!

OHHH!

It landed on Mabel, and all her kids too.

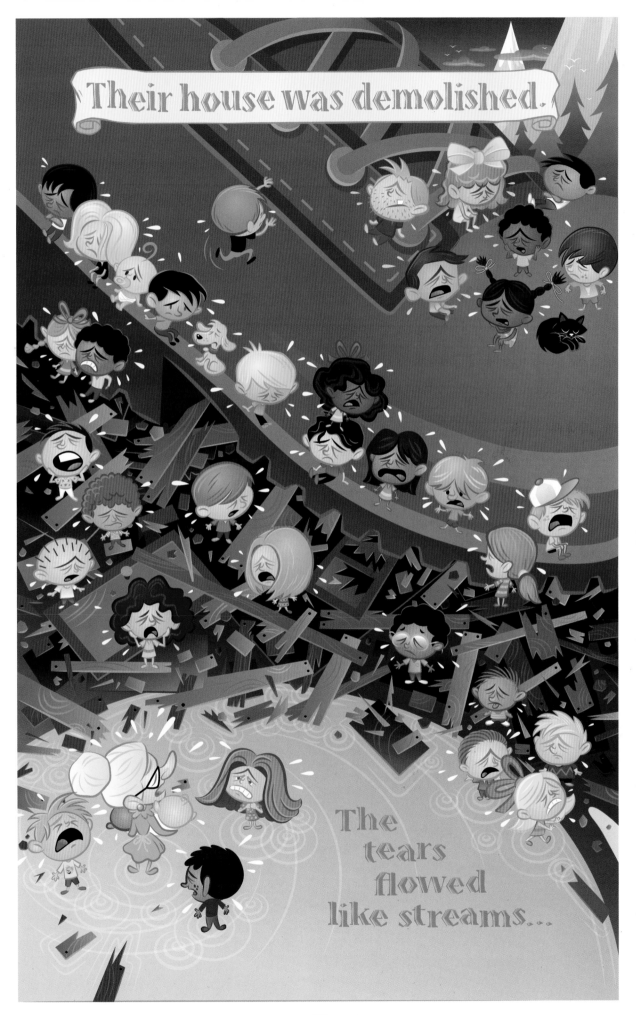

Their house was demolished.

The tears flowed like streams...

51

But the shoe was converted...

into the home of their dreams.

while watching the news.

"ON TOP of SPAGHETTI!"

STORY & ART: BILL "MAMA-MIA" MORRISON • COLORS AND LETTERS: SERBAN "CARBONARA" CRISTESCU

UH OH!

HERE IT COMES...!

♪ OOOHHH.... ON TOP OF ♪ SPAGHETTI...

♪ ALL COVERED ♪ WITH CHEESE...

AH-AH

♪ I LOST MY POOR ♪ MEATBALL...

♪ WHEN SOMEBODY ♪ SNEEZED!

AH-CHOO!

♪ IT ROLLED OFF THE TABLE, ♪ ♪ AND ONTO THE FLOOR... ♪

♪ AND THEN MY POOR MEATBALL, ROLLED RIGHT OUT THE DOOR! ♪

IT ROLLED IN THE GARDEN, AND UNDER A BUSH! AND THEN MY POOR MEATBALL, WAS NOTHING BUT MUSH!

THE MUSH WAS AS TASTY, AS TASTY COULD BE...

AND EARLY NEXT SUMMER, IT GREW INTO A TREE!

THE TREE WAS ALL COVERED, WITH BEAUTIFUL MOSS! IT GREW LOVELY MEATBALLS, AND TOMATO SAUCE!

SO IF YOU EAT SPAGHETTI, ALL COVERED WITH CHEESE, HOLD ONTO YOUR MEATBALL, AND DON'T EVER SNEEZE!

YOU KNOW, I JUST CAN'T GET OVER HOW MUCH JUNIOR LOVES SPAGHETTI!

WELL FROM NOW ON, WE'LL HAVE LASAGNA OR NOTHING!

THE END!

Starlight Starbright

STAR LIGHT,

STAR BRIGHT,

FIRST STAR I
SEE TONIGHT.

PHIL HESTER: ADAPTATION/LAYOUT   MIKE LAUGHEAD: ART   KEATON KOHL: INKS, COLORS, LETTERS

For any strange bug

Like a wasp

or a slug

Was subjected to Miss Muffet's affection

But a spider like this was perfect for Miss

And would add to her growing collection

Beetles that spray

And Mantids that pray

Her other "non traditional" pets

But her mother protested
And even suggested
That "spiders are venomous threats"

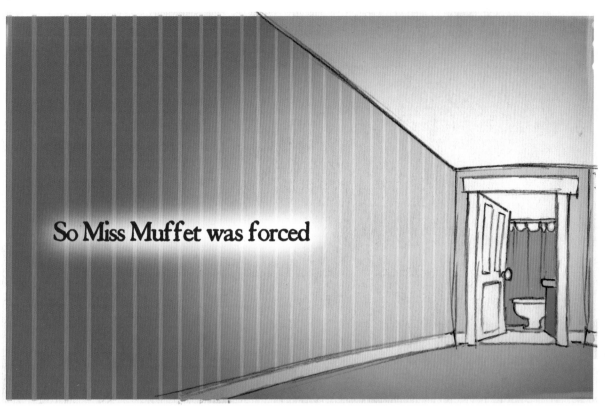

So Miss Muffet was forced

And her mother endorsed

The flushing of her new little pet

With the bug on the brink
To the left of the sink
She waved as the spider got wet

The End
by Royden Lepp

This is...

the house that jack built

Loosely adapted by **Neil Kleid** and **Fernando Pinto**

This is the house that Jack built.

These are the boys
That live in the house that Jack built.

These are the toys
Thrown by the boys
That live in the house that Jack built.

These are the neighbor kids
Who bring more toys
Just like the ones
Thrown by the boys
That live in the house that Jack built.

These are the parents
That raised the kids
Who tossed their toys
Just like the boys
That live in the house that Jack built.

This is the grill (gas, not coal!)
Owned by the neighbors
That raised the kids
Who threw their toys
Just like the boys
That live in the house that Jack built.

Dinner's served! And eaten whole,
Cooked by the grill (gas, not coal)
Owned by the neighbors
That raised the kids
Who threw their toys
Just like the boys
That live in the house that Jack built.

These high school kids
Will rock n' roll
For a few hamburgers
Cooked well and whole
By the grill that's gas
And still not coal

Owned by the neighbors
That raised the kids
Who threw their toys
Just like the boys
That live in the house that Jack built.

These are guitars
Played full blast
By high school kids
Who rocked n' rolled
After eating burgers from the grill

Owned by the neighbors
That raised the kids
Who threw their toys
Just like the boys
That live in the house that Jack built.

The party's loud
And growing fast
Thanks to music
Played full blast
By high school kids
That rocked the block
And ate the food

Cooked on the grill
Owned by the neighbors
That raised the kids
Who —oh, the toys!
Just like the boys
That live in the house that Jack built

Someone called the cops at last
To stop the noise and stop it fast!
And music, loud and played full blast
By high school kids
That rocked the block
And ate the food

Cooked on the grill
Owned by the neighbors
That raised the kids
Who threw their toys
Just like the boys
That live in the house that Jack built.

Here's our story's final cast
Cops joining in to make it last
This crazy party's quite a blast
With rock and roll that's loud and fast
Played by kids that rocked the block
And ate the food

Cooked on the grill
Owned by the neighbors
That raised the kids
Who threw their toys
Just like the boys
That live in the house that Jack built.

This is the hotel room
Quiet and cheap
Where poor old Jack
Can get some sleep
Far from the party
Going full blast
And rock and roll
That's loud and fast

By high school kids
That rock the block
And eat the food
Cooked on a grill
Owned by the neighbors
Who raised some kids
That threw their toys
Just like those boys

But here there's not
A bit of noise

Like the noise at the
house that Jack built.

THE FOX and THE CAT

RE-WRITTEN BY: NIKKI DY-LIACCO
DRAWN BY: MAY ANN LICUDINE

THE CAT ALWAYS WANTED TO MEET MR. FOX. SHE HEARD SO MUCH ABOUT HIM...

MR FOX IS THE MOST INTELLIGENT OF US ALL!

DID YOU SEE HIS LATEST GADGET?

HE HAS THE BEST-LOOKING CLOTHES!

HE IS THE COOLEST FOX IN ALL THE WOODS!

SHE HEARD ALL THE STORIES AND PRAISES. BUT NEVER SAW HIM FACE TO FACE. THE CAT IMAGINED WHAT IT WOULD BE LIKE WHEN SHE FINALLY GOT TO MEET HIM...

PERHAPS THEY WOULD EXCHANGE HELLOS, SHAKE HANDS, ENJOY A CONVERSATION AND BECOME GOOD FRIENDS.

THEN IT FINALLY HAPPENED ONE DAY THAT THE CAT MET MR. FOX.

HELLO, MY DEAR MR. FOX. I'VE HEARD SO MUCH ABOUT YOU! HOW ARE YOU TODAY?

SHIFF.

OH, YOU POOR BEARD LICKER, YOU SPOTTED FOOL, YOU HUNGRY MOUSE HUNTER. WHAT WERE YOU THINKING?

YOU HAVE SOME NERVE ASKING ME HOW I AM! WHAT DO YOU KNOW? HOW MANY TRICKS DO YOU UNDERSTAND?

PFFFFTTT!!! OH WELL...

THAT'S NOT ALL— LOOK HERE, I HAVE A MAGIC CAMOUFLAGE CLOAK THAT MAKES ME DISAPPEAR!

SWISH!

HEY WHAT HAPPENED?... WRAP??

I CAN'T... SEE...!

OUCH!

TOINK!

OH WELL. A-HEM.

YOU HAVEN'T SEEN ANYTHING YET. I'VE ONLY SHOWN YOU THE FIRST FIVE AMONG MY HUNDRED-AND-ONE TRICKS. OH, I DO FEEL SORRY FOR YOU. HI-HI-HI!

COME WITH ME AND I WILL TEACH YOU HOW ONE CAN ESCAPE FROM THE DOGS.

THESE ROCKETS CAN BLAST ME OUT OF HERE!

VROOOMM

UP, UP AND AWAY!!!

BBZZ...

POOF!

UH OH.

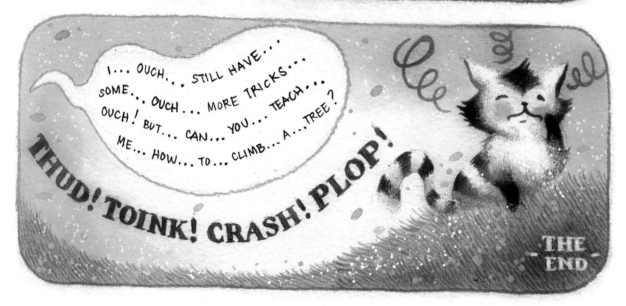

I... OUCH... STILL HAVE... SOME... OUCH... MORE TRICKS... OUCH! BUT... CAN... YOU... TEACH... ME... HOW... TO... CLIMB... A... TREE?

THUD! TOINK! CRASH! PLOP!

THE END

Pippi Van Wrinkles

Pippi! Hold still, you little...

I will be just the prettiest girl at Olaf's party...

...and we are going to play my favorite game - **Talk Show!**

Do I need more make-up?

Once upon a time there was a kingdom called Minny-soda which was known for its many lakes and its cute-as-a-button families! And there lived a little girl named **Pippi Van Wrinkles!**

And Pippi loved to **talk** - especially about herself!

Wolfamina's Beauty and Bowl

I'm prettier than Marcy...and I'm prettier than Ingrid...and I'm prettier than Sonya...

And I'm smarter than Olaf...and...

And I'm more graceful than Brandee...and I'm...

Oof!

And...Here's **Pippi!**

Un-huh.

Story and script: Len Strazewski Story, art, letters & colors: Paul Fricke Colors: Mary Fricke

The Real Princess

Story: Alexander Grecian

Art: Christian Ward

Once upon a castle...

There was a lonely prince who set out to search his kingdom for the pure and worthy princess who might win his heart.

While his mother, the queen, stayed home and worried about him.

As a young woman, the queen had married for love, rather than for money and, although her kingdom was not a rich one, she was happy.

MOOO

She worried that her prince would never find a princess as pure and as worthy as the queen herself had been in her youth.

The queen waited many months, but her son did not return.

Meanwhile, she bartered for the castle's daily needs.

For fabric, for grain, and even for livestock.

And what she had to barter with was a small quantity of magic beans that had been her dowry when she married.

One night, not long after the prince had gone in search of his one true love, there came a knock at the castle door.

It was a delicate knock and was barely heard over the sound of the storm.

The girl at the door claimed to be a travelling princess, looking for her one true love.

She hated to be wet, the girl said, and hoped to find a warm dry bed for the night.

The queen was suspicious of the girl, but didn't want to turn her away. So she made up a bed in a room at the top of the castle.

And placed a hard dry bean under the bottom-most mattress.

To test the girl's claim, the queen piled twenty mattress, plus one, on the bed...

If the girl was truly a pure and worthy princess, she would feel the bean, despite the one-and-twenty mattresses, and she would pass a sleepless night.

MOOO

The princess (yes, she was a real princess) was still a bit damp from the rain and she could not dry her eyes.

She was quite sad because she had been searching for many months and could not find a man she would call her one true love.

But the girl did finally sleep and, as she slept, her tears soaked through twenty mattresses, plus one.

The tears of the real princess watered that magic bean all through the night.

And the bean grew...

And grew.

Until the next morning, when the princess awoke...

And found herself in a kingdom above the clouds.

Where she finally found her one true love, a prince who was quite large.

And who could keep the princess safe and dry forever.

As the princess began her fulfilling new life above the clouds, and as the morning dawned below...

LET THE CONTEST *BEGIN!*

CHOMP! CHOMP! CHOMP!

GAH!

CHOMP!

CHOMP!

CHOMP!

CHOMP!

THE TORTOISE AND THE HARE BY JOSHUA WILLIAMSON AND VICENTE "VINNY" NAVARRETE

THE STRANGE FEAST

a tale by THE BROTHERS GRIMM
adapted by JILL THOMPSON

A BLOOD SAUSAGE AND A LIVER SAUSAGE HAD BEEN FRIENDS FOR SOME TIME...

PLEASE DINE WITH ME AT MY HOME, LIVER SAUSAGE!

AT DINNER TIME, THE LIVER SAUSAGE MERRILY SET OUT FOR THE BLOOD SAUSAGE'S HOUSE.

♪

BUT WHEN SHE WALKED THROUGH THE DOORWAY, SHE SAW ALL KINDS OF STRANGE THINGS.

!

WELCOME! WELCOME!

WHAT IS ALL THA—

OH TUT TUT!

...WHAT'S THAT?

THAT WAS PROBABLY MY MAID GOSSIPING WITH SOMEONE ON THE STAIRS...

...HAVE I SHOWN YOU MY NEW TEA SERVICE?

THIS WAY, DEAR!!

SUCH CURIOUS THINGS

SO ODD

OH MY

VERY STRANGE

EXCUSE ME FOR A MOMENT, DEAR, I MUST GO INTO THE KITCHEN AND LOOK AFTER THE MEAL...

TO CHECK TO SEE THAT EVERYTHING IS IN ORDER AND THAT NOTHING HAS — YOU KNOW — FALLEN INTO THE ASHES...

LET ME WARN YOU, LIVER SAUSAGE, YOU'RE IN A BLOODY MURDEROUS TRAP! YOU'D BETTER GET OUT OF HERE QUICKLY—

IF YOU VALUE YOUR LIFE!

THE LIVER SAUSAGE DID NOT HAVE TO THINK TWICE ABOUT THIS,

IF I WOULD HAVE CAUGHT YOU... I WOULD HAVE HAD YOU!!

FIN

I'M NOT TRYING TO BE "SNIDE", SIR. JUST ANSWER THE QUESTIONS, PLEASE.

"I'M OVER HEEERE, SIR"... SHEESH.

LIKE I CAN SEE WHERE YOU ARE.

RUDE.

FINE.

ME AN MY COUSINS LARRY AN' JIM, WE WAS OUT HOPPIN' AROUND.

ALLS WE WANTED WAS SOME PIE.

I MEAN, SHE JUST LEFT IT ON THE WINDOW LEDGE.

TO US MICE, THAT MEANS "FREE"

NOW, IT WAS NIGHT, AND...

WAIT...

...YOU THINK BECAUSE THE FARMER'S WIFE LEFT HER PIE OUT, THAT MEANS ITS "FREE"?

This is the plaintiff, Gladys Chacoby.
She was cleaning the gutters of her modest gingerbread house
when ALL OF A SUDDEN these two gluttonous beasts ran
out of the forest and devoured her beautiful home.
She is suing for $5,000, to cover
the cost of damages to her home.

PLAINTIFF

DEFENDANTS

Here are the defendants, Hansel and Gretel Klosterkemper.
These two dimwits didn't really comment much on what happened;
but after devouring three boxes of donuts at the police station,
murmured something about eating all of their bread crumbs
and still being hungry. They are accused of literally
eating an old woman out of house and home.

THE PEOPLE VS. HANSEL & GRETEL™

BY: JEREMY R. SCOTT

All rise!
The honorable
Judge Dumpty
presiding.

You may be seated.
Okay, Ms. Chacoby,
what happened?

RUSTY

JUDGE
DUMPTY

There I was, having the time of my life, cleaning my gutters—

It was horrible, your Honor. HORRIBLE. It was a beautiful, sunny day in the forest, so I decided to do some spring cleaning.

—when these two monstrous brutes came charging out of the forest.

They devoured my sugar-cookie siding and tore off my gumdrop shutters!

They tore out all of my licorice lattices and penny-candy nails as they destroyed my walls.

In a matter of minutes, I lost everything I had ever cherished!

SNORING BEAUTY

Kristen Simon
STORY

Seth Damoose
ART

Paul Little
COLORS

Ed Dukeshire
LETTERS

ONCE UPON A TIME, THERE WAS A KING AND QUEEN WHO HAD AT LAST BEEN BLESSED WITH A BEAUTIFUL DAUGHTER.

WE SHALL NAME HER *ROSE!*

THEY THREW A JOYOUS FEAST, BUT ONLY HAD ENOUGH GOLDEN PLATES TO INVITE 12 OF THE 13 WISE WOMEN.

THE PRINCESS WAS BLESSED BY 11 OF THE WOMEN, WHEN THE UNINVITED 13TH WOMAN CAME IN AND DECLARED THAT IN HER 15TH YEAR, THE PRINCESS WOULD PRICK HER FINGER ON A SPINDLE AND FALL DOWN DEAD!

YOU PICKED THE *WRONG* LADY TO LEAVE OFF THE GUEST LIST!

THE 12TH WOMAN HAD YET TO ANNOUNCE HER BLESSING, BUT COULD NOT UNDO THE CURSE, ONLY SOFTEN IT SO THAT SHE REMAINED ASLEEP UNTIL A PRINCE AWAKENED HER.

I'M *NOT* THAT GREAT AT THIS YET...

THE PRINCESS TURNS 15, AND SURE ENOUGH, THE CURSE COMES TO PASS.

WHAT NO ONE HAD COUNTED ON WAS THE LOUD SNORING THAT CAME FROM THE TINY PRINCESS WHILE SHE SLEPT!

CAN YOU *ROLL HER OVER* OR SOMETHING?!

THE PRINCESS BECAME KNOWN AS *BRIAR ROSE* FOR THE THORNY ROSE BUSHES THAT GREW AROUND HER CASTLE, MAKING IT HARD FOR PRINCES TO COME AND RESCUE HER.

MAKE IT STOP! MAKE IT *STOP!!*

HOWEVER, THE PRINCESSES SNORING WAS SO LOUD, NO ONE COULD GET CLOSE TO HER FOR FEAR OF GOING DEAF!

EVENTUALLY, THE KING AND QUEEN HAD TO MOVE OUT OF THE CASTLE TO GET SOME PEACE AND QUIET.

SHE DOESN'T EVEN SOUND *HUMAN*!

SNNRRRRRKK!

BUT STRANGELY, THE EMPTIER THE CASTLE WAS, THE LOUDER THE SNORING BECAME!

SNOOORRKKK

IT WAS SO LOUD, THAT EVENTUALLY THE TOWNSPEOPLE MOVED AWAY, LEAVING THE ENTIRE TOWN DESERTED, ASIDE FROM THE SNORING PRINCESS.

ALONE IN THE KINGDOM, THE PRINCESS SNORED ON, OBLIVIOUS TO THE TERRIBLE NOISE SHE WAS CREATING AND WITH LITTLE HOPE OF EVER BEING AWAKENED!

GRRROONKKK!

HUNDREDS OF YEARS PASSED AND HER SNORING GREW SO LOUD THAT THE CASTLE WALLS BEGAN TO CRACK...

...SO LOUD THAT THE CASTLE ITSELF BEGAN TO CRUMBLE AND FALL...

SNOOOOREEEE

CARASSSHH

...SO LOUD THAT THE ENTIRE VILLAGE FELL INTO RUIN!

SNNNARRRRKKKK

AND YOU'D *THINK* THAT WOULD BE THE END OF BRIAR ROSE, *WOULDN'T* YOU?

WHAT *IS* THAT AWFUL NOISE?

BUT THE SNORING WENT ON AND ON... AND IS PROBABLY GOING ON STILL.

PRINCE

The End

The Little Mermaid

Written by *Peter David*
Illustrated by *Juan Ferreyra*
Lettered by *Johnny Lowe*

In the deepest part of the ocean resided the castle of the king of the sea. Now the king had been a widower for many years, and his old mother kept house for him...

...and tended to his six lovely daughters, five of whom were shy and retiring and enjoyed the wonders of the sea...

But the sixth, the littlest of the mermaids, would sit in the garden and gaze upon the statue of a human that she had salvaged from a sunken ship.

She had heard many stories of the surface, for on a mermaid's fifteenth birthday, she is allowed to sit upon the rocks and gaze upon the world of man.

finally, her fifteenth birthday arrived, and she clambered upon the rocks and looked in wonderment upon the surface world.

And she saw, out upon the ocean, a great sailing ship. There was music and celebration coming from within, and she was drawn to it.

The waves were becoming great chops, and she thought it good sport to ride one up toward the ship so she could see it more clearly.

And there she saw the birthday of a young and handsome prince being joyously celebrated.

He was so handsome, and filled with joy, and the Little Mermaid was immediately smitten with him.

And then a fierce storm rolled in, and the sailors scrambled, and the people were sorely afraid. And then...

The prince had been so busy helping others to the lifeboats that he was unable to escape himself and plunged into the depths.

Remembering that humans could not survive beneath the water, she hastened to his side...

And brought him to safety, leaving him only with the memory of a fleeting glimpse of a young woman's face...

...and a gentle voice assuring him that he would be safe.

Try as she might, the Little Mermaid could not cleanse the image of the prince from her mind, and knew she had to be with him.

And so she sought out the one individual who could possibly help her...

The Sea Witch, who dwelt in the foulest part of the ocean, in a house made of the bones of shipwrecked men.

I CAN PROVIDE YOU A POTION THAT WILL GIVE YOU *LEGS*. BUT YOU WILL HAVE TO GIVE ME YOUR TONGUE IN PAYMENT...

...AND IF YOUR PRINCE BREAKS YOUR HEART, THEN YOU WILL BE TRANSFORMED INTO *FOAM*.

CUT OUT MY TONGUE, THEN, FOR I AM RESOLVED THAT I CANNOT LIVE WITHOUT HIM.

Unaware of the sacrifice the Little Mermaid was undergoing, the prince stared out to sea. The time for him to take a *wife* was drawing near, and although many beautiful maidens had presented themselves to him...

...he could not forget the face of the beautiful girl who had rescued him.

And then, to his amazement...

... from the surf emerged she who had--

OOOOOOFFF!!

OH, BANDAFTIK!

BERRY BUNNY!

WH-WHAT DID YOU SAY?

BAY RIBE BERE!

HUH?

RIBE BERE! DON'T BOOVE! BAY RIBE BERE!

RIPE... BEER?

WHAT?

Hoping that he would attend to her instructions to "stay right there," she returned to the sea witch to issue a complaint and demand legs with feet.

YOU... YOU CAME BACK!

I WAS BEGINNING TO WONDER, IT WAS TAKING SO--

UHM...

BUNUVA...

YOU, UH... YOU GOT CHAIR LEGS THERE.

IS THAT, YOU KNOW... *HEREDITARY?* BECAUSE THAT COULD BE A FACTOR IN--

BON'T BOOVE! BAY BERE!

YOU KEEP TALKING ABOUT BEER, AND I JUST...I'M NOT GETTING WHAT YOU...

And so she returned to the sea to confront the witch and this time make sure to demand *human* legs with feet...

...and ankles, and knees, and Achilles tendons intact, and everything *else* she could think of.

Unfortunately...

118

... she forgot to specify *gender*.

BIF IF BIDIKULIF!

BAY BERE...

NO, YOU KNOW WHAT? FORGET IT. I'M JUST...LOOK, NO **OFFENSE**...

...I DON'T KNOW WHAT YOUR **DEAL** IS, BUT THE WHOLE PACKAGE, WITH THE FREAKY LEGS AND THE SPEECH IMPEDIMENT AND THE BEER FIXATION...

...IT'S JUST WEIRDING ME OUT TOO MUCH.

I'M SURE YOU'RE NICE AND EVERYTHING, BUT YOU KNOW WHAT THEY SAY...

...THERE'S PLENTY OF FISH IN THE SEA.

And so it was that the Little Mermaid's heart was broken. And yet, with all that, still she wanted to be with her prince...

...and so, even as she began to transform into foam, she sent a silent prayer to the gods asking that she be allowed to be with her prince, and he would love her.

And the gods answered her prayer.

"TO THE *PRINCE* AND HIS BEAUTIFUL *BRIDE!*"

THANK YOU ALL, ON BEHALF OF BOTH MYSELF AND MY NEW WIFE.

AND MY APPRECIATION TO THE BREWMASTER FOR THIS FINE *BEER!*

IN PARTICULAR, I LOVE THE *FOAM!*

STUPID GODS.

THE END

120

THE END

Spanking Robots

written by Laini Taylor
art & lettering by Jim Di Bartolo

Once upon a time there was a robot-maker named Geppetto.

He spent all his time with his cold steel creations, and he was lonely.

One day he fashioned a robot boy out of scraps.

I'm going to call you Wingnut.

AND I WILL CALL YOU FATHER.

Wingnut was like a son to Geppetto, and for a few days, Geppetto forgot his loneliness.

But there was a problem.

I LOVE YOU, FATHER.

Everything Wingnut did, Geppetto had programmed him to do.

He wasn't a son at all--

--he was more of a wind-up toy.

I LOVE YOU, FATHER.

I LOVE YOU, FATHER.

-CLICK-

-CLICK-

I LOVE YOU, FA--

126

Geppetto made a wish.

I wish Wingnut was *alive*.

The Blue Fairy, passing by, heard his wish and granted it.

As soon as Geppetto woke up the next morning, he realized something was different about Wingnut.

Pull my finger.

Um, what? Sure. Why?

yank

PIRRRFFFFFT

Oh! ...WINGNUT! What the--?!

AND SO MATCHSTICK AND HER DOG GAVE A VERY EXCITING DEMO OF THEIR PRODUCT...

...THOUGH THEY LEARNED THE HARD WAY NOT TO PLAY WITH FIRE.

SPLASH!

EXCUSE ME, LITTLE LADY.

I HAVE REPORTS OF A JUVENILE DELINQUENT SETTING FIRES AROUND HERE. HAVE YOU SEEN SOMEBODY MATCHING THAT DESCRIPTION?

GASP, THAT MUST'VE BEEN ME, BUT IT WAS ONLY AN ACCIDENT SIR! I'M ONLY TRYING TO SELL MY MATCHSTICKS.

I SEE, WELL YOU'RE A BIT SHORT, MAYBE IF YOU WERE A LITTLE TALLER YOU'D HAVE AN EASIER TIME GETTING EVERYONE'S ATTENTION.

IF I WERE TALLER...

YEAH, THAT'D BE PERFECT! THANKS MISTER FIREMAN!

-THE END-

GAMBOLING GOATS OF GRUFF!

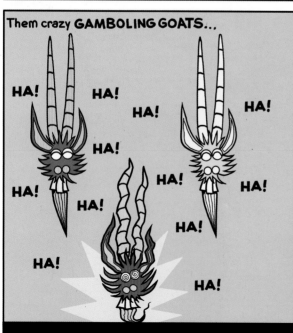

Them crazy GAMBOLING GOATS...

HA!
HA!
HA!
HA!
HA!
HA!
HA!
HA!
HA!
HA!
HA!
HA!

...was making a very loud rumpus!

HA!
HA!
HA!
HA!
HA!
HA!
HA!
HA!
HA!
HA!

GAMBOLING GOATS OF GRUFF WOKE UP THE TROLLLLLLL...

When we come to, they all was gone! No **TROLL**. No **GAMBOLING GOATS**. It was hard to believe we was still alive!

We never did figure out what had happened.

But we was so happy we kicked up a ruckus the whole night long.

And it was a mighty good time.

Cinderella

Once upon a time, there was a widower who took a new wife. From his first marriage, he had a beautiful daughter—known throughout the village for her kindness and charm.

His new wife had two daughters of her own, known throughout the village as well—but for their cruelty and malice. They and their mother forced the widower's girl to do all the house chores, working her through all hours of the night.

When she finished, they made her sit in the cinders that came in from the fire stove, nicknaming her "Cinderella."

story: Nick Spencer

Then one day, a handsome prince invited all the young women in the land to a grand ball, so that he could find a wife of his own.

Loyal Subjects,

I'm having a totally awesome party at the palace. It'll be off the chain, seriously. And I'd love to invite all you fine ladies to come.

xoxo Prince Charming

P.S. Wear something hot.

art: Rodin Esquejo

Cinderella dreamed of attending the ball and finding true love, but her evil Stepmother and Stepsisters forbade her from going—and instead demanded she stay home and do more work.

That night, though, after they had departed for the gala, something magical happened...

letters: Thomas Mauer

148

NO MORE TEARS, SWEET-HEARTED CINDERELLA! I AM YOUR FAIRY GODMOTHER, AND I AM HERE TO MAKE YOUR WISHES COME TRUE!

WOW! YOU MEAN LIKE A GENIE?

WHAT? NO, NO, *DISGUSTING*--GENIES LIVE IN BOTTLES! DO I LOOK LIKE I LIVE IN A BOTTLE? I TOLD YOU, I AM YOUR FAIRY GODMOTHER!

SO YOU KNOW MY PARENTS? IT'S JUST--THEY NEVER MENTIONED ME HAVING A GODMOTHER...

NO, NO, NO, SILLY CHILD-- IT'S JUST AN EXPRE--

LOOK, IT'S VERY SIMPLE. EVERYONE HAS A FAIRY GODMOTHER LOOKING AFTER THEM.

DON'T YOU MEAN A GUARDIAN ANGEL?

WELL, I NEVER!

LISTEN TO ME VERY CAREFULLY, I AM YOUR *FAIRY GODMOTHER!* EVERYONE HAS A FAIRY GOD-MOTHER THAT TAKES CARES OF THEM IN TIMES OF GREAT NEED!

NEVER HEARD OF IT. CAN I SEE SOME ID?

≈SIGH≈ DO YOU WANT YOUR DREAMS TO COME TRUE OR NOT?

I GET THREE OF THEM, RIGHT?

OH, FOR HEAVEN'S SAKE!

HMM... TOO MILEY.

TOO SELINA.

UGH--TOO LINDSAY AFTER A BREAKUP-EY.

THAT'S IT! *THAT'S IT!* PERFECT!

FINALLY! NOW, CAN WE GET GOING?

OF COURSE! I CAN'T WAIT FOR EVERYONE TO SEE--OUCH!

WHAT IS IT? WHAT'S WRONG?

IT'S JUST... THESE SHOES! WHAT ARE THESE THINGS MADE OF?!

WHY, THOSE ARE GLASS SLIPPERS!

GLASS?! HOW AM I SUPPOSED TO WALK AROUND IN SHOES MADE OUT OF GLASS?! YOU REALIZE I HAVE TO DANCE IN THESE THINGS, RIGHT?!

BUT-BUT-THEY'RE ONE OF KIND! THAT WAY IF YOU'RE SEPARATED BY CHANCE, THE PRINCE WILL KNOW--

ONE OF KIND? HOW ABOUT SOME CUSTOM-ORDER DESIGNER HEELS THEN? THE PRINCE WILL DEFINITELY REMEMBER THOSE! OR AT LEAST, I WILL...

≶GROAN≶ FINE. NOW COME ALONG, YOUR CHARIOT AWAITS, M'LADY!

OH, BOY.

WHAT?

IT'S...A PUMPKIN.

WELL, YES. I HAVE MAGICALLY TRANSFORMED YOUR PUMPKIN INTO A CARRIAGE! YOU LIKE IT?

I DON'T MEAN TO BE RUDE, I REALLY DON'T, BUT, WELL--YOU UNDERSTAND THIS ISN'T A HALLOWEEN PARTY RIGHT?

HEY, MAYBE YOU COULD MAKE A STRETCH LIMO OUT OF MY CELL PHONE, YEAH?!

≥SIGH≤ I DON'T GET PAID ENOUGH FOR THIS.

The End!

Bios

Bill Alger *(page 49)* is a Brooklyn-based artist who has illustrated titles including SCOOBY DOO, DEXTER'S LABORATORY, TONKA TOUGH TRUCKS and HAMTARO. He also wrote and illustrated JUNE COMICS.

Laura Allred *(Cover and page 155)* is an award-winning artist in her own right. She works primarily with her husband, Mike, and is one of the most respected colorists in the field.

Mike Allred *(Cover and page 155)* first tasted success in the comics field with his wildly popular MADMAN series, which is currently being developed for a live action movie with filmmaker Robert Rodriguez. Mike has drawn SANDMAN, created X-MEN, and has worked on every major comic book character including BATMAN, SUPERMAN, SPIDER-MAN, IRON MAN, and the HULK.

Grant Bond *(page 9)* is a cartoonist who created and illustrated THE ABSURD ADVENTURES OF ARCHIBALD AARDVARK series for Shadowline in 2009. He is best-known for REVERE: REVOLUTION IN SILVER, just in case your U.S. History teacher left out the part where Paul Revere mangled a werewolf.

Serban Cristescu *(page 55)* is best known for his innovative contributions as Designer for Matt Groening's hit TV series, FUTURAMA, and for his design and coloring work for Bongo Entertainment's cornucopia of FUTURAMA and THE SIMPSONS books and calendars.

Marie Cruz *(page 30)* is a writer of young adult novels and picture books, a scientist, a proud mother of two teens and the wife of a Jedi knight (her husband's name is Obi!). Reading is one of her favorite things to do. She also loves to knit. It's a great remedy for writer's block.

Seth Damoose *(page 109)* has worked on a variety of projects, such as BRAT-HALLA, STEAMPUNK FAERIES, and SPOOK'D. However, Seth is best known for the Shadowline series I HATE GALLANT GIRL, and BOMB QUEEN PRESENTS: ALL GIRL COMICS.

Tim Daniel *(Cover graphics and logo)* has been contributing logos and production designs to the covers and interiors of many comics over the last several years including, EXISTENCE 2.0/3.0, FORGETLESS, POWERS, SKY PIRATES OF NEO TERRA, SHUDDERTOWN and SCARLET. He lives in Montana with his wife and daughter.

Peter David *(page 113)*, writer of stuff, has produced over a thousand comic books and seventy novels. He currently writes X-FACTOR and STEPHEN KING'S DARK TOWER for Marvel Comics, and FALLEN ANGEL for IDW. He named his third daughter "Ariel" after the Little Mermaid and apologizes profusely to both of them.

Camilla d'Errico *(page 16)* lives the double life of character creator and comic artist/painter. She has expanded her style into designer toys, fashion, merchandise, and videogames. She has distinguished herself through her ability to seamlessly weave comic art and manga. One of her most recent works is SKY PIRATES OF NEO TERRA for Image Comics.

Jim Di Bartolo (page 125) is an illustrator that has collaborated on three novels and one graphic novel (THE DROWNED, through Image Comics) with his wife, writer Laini Taylor. Their most recent collaboration (LIPS TOUCH: THREE TIMES) was a finalist for the National Book Award. He lives in Portland, Oregon with his wife and baby daughter.

Nikki Dy-Liacco (page 73) is a marketing professional from the Philippines and currently lives in Singapore. She has authored three children's books since 2005 including THE YELLOW PAPERCLIP WITH BRIGHT PURPLE SPOTS, her first book with May Ann Licudine and wishes she had more time to daydream, watch clouds and write stories.

Rodin Esquejo (page 148) is a freelance artist based out of the Bay Area, California. Since receiving his B.A. in Graphic Design, he has been working steadily on projects for Hasbro, com.X, Vineyard Press, as well as private commissions.

Juan Ferreyra (page 113) is an Argentinean illustrator whose work includes Shadowline's LAZARUS, EMISSARY and SMALL GODS and Dark Horse's REX MUNDI. He was also featured in JIM VALENTINO'S SHADOWHAWK #13: PAST LIVES, drawing the first female ShadowHawk.

Paul Fricke (page 81) is a freelance cartoonist of twenty-five years, working in comics and illustration for various applications. His first childrens book, NIGHT OF THE BEDBUGS is now available from Image/Silverline Books. He lives in Minnesota with his wife and two daughters; a family of artists.

Alexander Grecian (page 88) wrote the graphic novels SEVEN SONS and SQUEAK! and continues to write the critically-acclaimed PROOF series. He sleeps reasonably well near Kansas City with his one true love and their son.

Brian Haberlin (page 121) and his studio do work for Image, Marvel and DC Comics. Brian is known as a WITCHBLADE co-creator, and also for his Avalon Studios titles such as ARIA and HELLCOP and his recent run on SPAWN with David Hine. He is currently working on a new 250 page graphic novel called ANOMALY to come out later this year, he writes for 3DWorld Magazine, and teaches at Minneapolis College of Art and Design.

Phil Hester's (page 58) work has been featured in: SWAMP THING, GREEN ARROW, NIGHTWING, ANT-MAN, THE COFFIN, DEEP SLEEPER, and the Eisner-nominated THE WRETCH. Current work includes: FIREBREATHER for Image Comics, and THE DARKNESS for Top Cow. Phil lives in small town Iowa with his wife and two children.

Neil Kleid (page 67) is a Xeric Award winning cartoonist who authored NINETY CANDLES, a graphic novella about life, death, legacy and comics; Neil also wrote the series THE INTIMIDATORS for Shadowline, and has been featured in the award-winning Image anthologies COMIC BOOK TATTOO and POPGUN. He also writes the webcomic ACTION, OHIO on the Shadowline webcomics hub.

Keaton Kohl (page 58) has a B.F.A. from the Kansas City Art Institute. He loves writing, inking, coloring, lettering and prop building. Currently he is the Head of Make-up for the four largest haunted houses in the country. In his free time he inks pencils for artists Mike Laughead and Jake Schmidt.

Mike Laughead (page 58) sits in a small room and draws pictures. Some of those pictures entertain his 2 young daughters. When not entertaining, Mike also does freelance illustration and comics. He is currently drawing a children's picture book and trying to be a good husband.

Royden Lepp (page 60) was born at a very young age in Brandon, Manitoba Canada. He grew up in British Columbia and was trained in 2d animation at the Vancouver Film School. Royden currently lives with his wife in the Seattle area, working in games and drinking coffee. His other works include the DAVID: THE SHEPHERD'S SONG, and the BARNABAS BEAR series.

May Ann Licudine (page 73) is a Filipino freelance illustrator and visual artist that lives in La Union, Philippines. She is a graduate in Certificate of Fine Arts at the University of the Philippines, Baguio City. She has competed and won in some prestigious art competitions both locally and internationally. Her illustrations have been exhibited in various galleries in Europe and the USA.

Larry Marder (page 141) released the first issue of BEANWORLD in 1985. He later joined the comic book circus full-time as the Executive Director of Image Comics and later President of McFarlane Toys. In 2007, he retired from business and returned to creating BEANWORLD full-time. He lives in Orange County, California, with his wife, Cory, and their two cats, Olive and Chipper.

Derek McCulloch (page 135) collaborated with artist Jimmie Robinson on the children's book T. RUNT! for Shadowline's younger readers imprint Silverline Books. His graphic novels for adults include STAGGER LEE, with Shepherd Hendrix; PUG, with Greg Espinoza; and GONE TO AMERIKAY, with Colleen Doran (coming from Vertigo in 2011).

Ted McKeever (page 145) is the Eisner-nominated creator behind such prominent works as TRANSIT, EDDY CURRENT, METROPOL and PLASTIC FORKS. More recently, he has worked on various DC and IDW titles, and contributed to Image's Tori Amos anthology, COMIC BOOK TATTOO. Currently, he is working on a brand new series called META 4, to be released through Shadowline in 2010.

Terry Moore (page 21) is an Eisner and Harvey Award winning cartoonist, best known for his self-published series, ECHO and STRANGERS IN PARADISE. In addition to his own books, Moore has worked with every major comic book publisher, writing and/or drawing for titles such as STAR WARS, RUNAWAYS, SPIDER-MAN LOVES MARY JANE, BUFFY THE VAMPIRE SLAYER and GEN 13.

Bill Morrison (page 55) has worked as an automotive illustrator, a Disney movie poster artist, a photo-realistic airbrush illustrator, and a merchandise artist for THE SIMPSONS. Since 1994, he has been creating comics and books for Matt Groening's Bongo Entertainment. Bill's current extracurricular project is LADY ROBOTIKA, which he co-created with Jane Wiedlin and is being released through Shadowline.

Scott Morse (page 100) is the creator of the Eisner and Ignatz Award nominated SOULWIND, as well as the graphic novels VISITATIONS, VOLCANIC REVOLVER, and MAGIC PICKLE for Oni Press and ANCIENT JOE for Dark Horse. In animation, Morse has worked as a character designer, storyboard artist, and art director for studios including Disney, Universal and Cartoon Network.

Dara Naraghi (page 9) lives in Columbus, Ohio and has written comics for kids and grown ups, including THE ABSURD ADVENTURES OF ARCHIBALD AARDVARK (Image), IGOR, and GHOSTBUSTERS. His favorite color is green, he has a hound dog named Duncan, and believe it or not, he likes brussel sprouts!

Vicente Navarrete (*page 93*), or 'Vinny' to his friends, illustrated DEAR DRACULA for Silverline Books, Shadowline's imprint for younger readers. He's also the writer and illustrator for his creator-owned book called KITE DAY.

Anthony Peruzzo (*page 135*) is an artist living in Minnesota. His work has been published by Image comics, Desperado Publishing and DC Comics' online division, Zuda comics.

Fernando Pinto (*page 67*) has worked on TALES OF THE TMNT, HACK/SLASH, POPGUN and URSA MINORS. You can find him nowadays working on his online graphic novel called WARPED! at warpedcomic.wordpress.com and at his website fernandopintoart.com. He'll like you if you're nice.

Whilce Portacio (*page 30*) became noted for his work on such Marvel titles as THE PUNISHER, X-FACTOR, and THE UNCANNY X-MEN. In 1992, Portacio left Marvel to co-found Image Comics with six other high-profile artists. Currently, he just wrapped up a run on SPAWN and is working on IMAGE UNITED with those same high profile artists from 1992 and will be launching his own Image series from it called FORTRESS.

Jeremy R. Scott (*page 106*) is the graphic artist on THE LAVA IS A FLOOR from Silverline Books, and also Silverline Books' first wordless picture book entitled PTA NIGHT.

Kristen K. Simon (*pages 24 and 109*) has been the Editor for Shadowline and Silverline Books since 2004, and has also authored two Silverline Books titles called BRUCE THE LITTLE BLUE SPRUCE and TIFFANY'S EPIPHANY. She is also the creator of ALL GIRL COMICS, and is the inspiration for the character "Editor Girl," who appears frequently in Shadowline comics.

Nick Spencer (*page 148*) is the writer of no less than four titles from Shadowline: The critically acclaimed EXISTENCE 2.0 and EXISTENCE 3.0, FORGETLESS, SHUDDERTOWN and the upcoming MORNING GLORIES.

Len Strazewski (*page 81*) has been writing comics for more than 20 years and is best known for JUSTICE SOCIETY OF AMERICA by DC Comics, PRIME by Malibu Ultraverse/Marvel Comics and TERROR TOTS by Caliber Comics. He is presently associate professor and acting chair of the Journalism Department at Columbia College Chicago.

Bryan Talbot (*page 16*) has worked on stories for JUDGE DREDD, BATMAN, HELLBLAZER, SANDMAN and FABLES and has written and drawn the graphic novels THE ADVENTURES OF LUTHER ARKWRIGHT, HEART OF EMPIRE, THE TALE OF ONE BAD RAT and ALICE IN SUNDERLAND. In 2009 he was awarded a Doctorate in Arts. His new book is GRANDVILLE, a steampunk detective thriller.

Laini Taylor (*page 125*) was a finalist for the National Book Award. She lives in Portland, Oregon with husband, Jim DiBartolo and new daughter Clementine Pie. Her novels for young people, DREAMDARK: BLACKBRINGER, DREAMDARK: SILKSINGER, and LIPS TOUCH: THREE TIMES have garnered starred reviews from Kirkus, Booklist and Publisher's Weekly.

Ben Templesmith (page 13) is a New York Times best-selling artist and writer most widely known for his work in the American comic book industry where he has received multiple nominations for the International Horror Guild Awards as well as the industry's top prize, the Eisner Award. As a creator, his most notable works have been 30 DAYS OF NIGHT (which has now spawned a major motion picture) and FELL. Currently Ben is working on his creator-owned title CHOKER through Image Comics.

Doug TenNapel (page 41) In addition to creating EARTHWORM JIM, Doug is also known for his work on graphic novels such as FLINK, MONSTER ZOO, and POWER UP. TenNapel is also the lead singer of an independent band called Truck and is currently working on a Cartoon Network Original called PHIBIAN MIKE.

Jill Thompson (page 98) is the creator of the critically acclaimed and Eisner Award-winning children's book SCARY GODMOTHER and as a comic book artist has garnered acclaim and multiple awards for her work on WONDER WOMAN, SWAMP THING, BLACK ORCHID and the award-winning title SANDMAN with Neil Gaiman.

Aaron Valentino (page 24) has been telling stories all his life, creating his first character at age 5 for Marvel's GUARDIANS OF THE GALAXY. His contribution here marks his first collaboration with his father. He is currently writing and illustrating his first graphic novel, LOGINIS.

Jim Valentino (page 24) In his 30 year career, Jim has worked for nearly every comic company as a writer, artist or both. He has won several awards, is a co-founder of Image Comics and the President/founder of Silverline Books. Jim is best known for such diverse creations as normalman, SHADOWHAWK, and A TOUCH OF SILVER among others.

Joel Valentino (page 129) Heavily influenced by manga and Anime, Joel is a college student in Southern California where he studies Japanese. An artist since childhood, his contribution here represents his first professionally published work.

Christian Ward (page 88) is currently found in London, often sports a beard and partakes in drawing of mysterious femme fatales, psychedelic mind clouds and men in capes. He co-created OLYMPUS from Image Comics and enjoys splashing pixels and paint around liberally.

Shannon Wheeler (page 26) is the creator of TOO MUCH COFFEE MAN. He won an Eisner and wrote an opera. He produces a weekly cartoon ironically titled "HOW TO BE HAPPY." He's cartooned for the print version of the Onion and the New Yorker. One can find his most recent cartoons on www.tmcm.com and www.act-i-vate.com. He lives in Portland, OR on a volcano with his kids, cats and chickens.

Shane White (page 38) at heart is a storyteller who exists on the comic fringe meandering in and out of styles and subjects that both challenge and suit his eclectic tastes. Some of his works include: NORTH COUNTRY, THE OVERMAN, COMIC BOOK TATTOO and THINGS UNDONE.

Joshua Williamson (page 93) writes comics, kids books and lives in Portland, home of big trees, rain, Oni Press, Dark Horse and Shadowline. He has been published by Shadowline; his credits include OVERLOOK, JOHNNY MONSTER and the children's book DEAR DRACULA, published by Shadowline's younger readers imprint Silverline Books.

If you enjoyed this book,
please join us at our web site:

www.silverlinebooks.com

for previews of our other fine publications
(see the next page)
plus puzzles, mazes, word searches,
downloadable coloring pages,
news of upcoming events,
author appearances
and other fun stuff!

We'll look forward to seeing you there!

Silverline Books is
dedicated to publishing quality, family-
friendly books that bridge the gap
between traditional storybooks and
graphic novels.

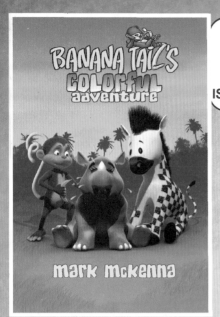

Mark McKenna

Banana Tail's Colorful Adventure
32 pages Hardcover
$12.99 Ages 4-8
ISBN: 978-1-60706-164-9

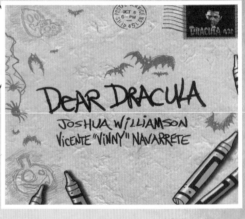

Paul Fricke

Night of the Bedbugs
32 pages Hardcover
$12.99 ages 4-8
ISBN: 978-1-60706-145-8

Dear Dracula
48 pages Hardcover
$7.99 Ages 4-8
ISBN: 978-1-58240-970-2

DEAR DRACULA
JOSHUA WILLIAMSON
VICENTE "VINNY" NAVARRETE

The Surreal Adventures of Edgar Allan Poo
96 pages Softcover
$9.99 Ages 12+
ISBN: 978-1-58240-816-3

T.Runt
40 pages Hardcover
$12.99 Ages 4-8
ISBN: 978-1-60706-074-1

By Derek McCulloch & Jimmie Robinson

The Surreal Adventures of Edgar Allan Poo II
96 pages Softcover
$12.99 Ages 12+
ISBN: 978-1-58240-975-7

The Lava Is A Floor!
32 pages Hardcover
$12.99 Ages 4-8
ISBN: 978-1-60706-123-6

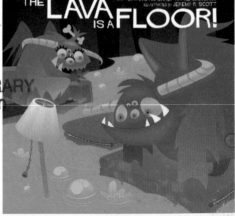

THE LAVA IS A FLOOR!